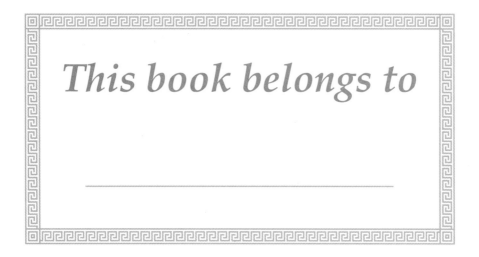

This book belongs to

_____

MY SUNNY DAY, ANY DAY
NURSERY RHYME BOOK

V. GILBERT BEERS
Illustrated by TIM O'CONNOR

THOMAS NELSON PUBLISHERS
Nashville

Published in Nashville, Tennessee, by Oliver-Nelson Books, a division of Thomas Nelson, Inc., Publishers, and distributed in Canada by Word Communications, Ltd., Richmond, British Columbia.

Printed in the United States of America.

ISBN 0–8407–9253–0

1   2   3   4   5   6   98   97   96   95   94   93

Table of Contents

Before you fall in love with this book . . .

Take time to read the following. It will help you understand the unique nature of this book and its adventures. You will better understand what you are reading and why it has been created this way.

You are about to enter into an adventure. There is no other quite like it. This book blends time-honored nursery rhymes with something new for today. And it visually interprets these with the best-selling Joyful Noise™ characters.

WHY NURSERY RHYMES?

Millions of parents were raised on, and have raised their children on, nursery rhymes. We and our children can quote most of the old classics because we have heard them hundreds of times.

Nursery rhymes are here to stay. That's why they are classics. But they have changed many times through the years. Once more, I have taken the liberty to slightly revise some of the classics to make them more understandable for your children. I have tried to keep the lilt, rhythm, rhyme, and quality that has made the classics endure. But it is time for another periodic revision, as well as for a few new rhymes. This book is a blend—classics, revised classics, and some new rhymes.

Nursery rhymes are best known for their rhythm and rhyme, as well as for the charming imagery so unique to this type of poem. Don't try to find the logic in the rhymes because they weren't written to be logical. We love them simply for what they are, and that's why they have been passed on for generations.

Most nursery rhymes do not have a story line either. But the imagery is so powerful they intrigue us anyway. They don't go anywhere. They aren't realistic and they aren't logical. But they have stirred the delight of several generations.

WHERE DID NURSERY RHYMES COME FROM?

Nobody knows. Children have listened to poems and rhymes for centuries. But, like fairy tales, these poems were not generally collected and published until the nineteenth century. Thus nursery rhymes and fairy tales were passed along orally. And in the telling, they must have changed from one generation to another.

In 1697, Charles Perrault collected some fairy tales without rhymes. John Newbery, who first published children's books in English, published a collection of fairy tales in 1729. And the Brothers Grimm are perhaps the most famous collector of fairy tales, compiling in the early 1800s what they had heard. But these collections were all of fairy tales without rhyme.

Some classic nursery rhymes were in circulation, though not in print, as early as the first part of the 1600s. Some say they are much older, but no one knows for sure.

Nursery rhymes that appeared in the 1800s were somewhat different from the same rhymes today. They have been edited and revised slightly in different collections. I have tried to present classics in their original form, returning to the nursery rhymes published in the 1800s. I have revised them only where it was necessary in order that the child of today could understand them.

WHY SOME NURSERY RHYMES ARE REVISED OR OMITTED FROM THIS BOOK

Some of the early nursery rhymes used words that your child would not understand because the words are not commonly used today. For example, in the rhyme I SAW A SHIP A-SAILING, one line says, "there were comfits in the cabin." I changed comfits (sweetmeats, sweets) to chocolates. This is not an exact synonym, but a specific sweetmeat or comfit common today.

In GOOSEY, GOOSEY, GANDER, there is a line that says Goosey wanders into "my lady's chamber." Children today would not understand that a chamber is just a room. I changed the line to: "and then over yonder" and the picture carries out where "over yonder" is.

In DIDDLE, DIDDLE, DUMPLING, the older rhymes spoke of John "going to bed with his stockings on." But what boy wears "stockings" today? Children better understand the terms *shoes* and *socks*.

Some nursery rhymes contained more violence than I care to put into a book for your children and my grandchildren. In GOOSEY, GOOSEY, GANDER, the second stanza says, "There I met an old man who wouldn't say his prayers; I took him by the left leg, and threw him down the stairs." This isn't exactly the best way to encourage an old man to pray! So I omitted that stanza from this book.

THREE BLIND MICE is not included in this book. I wanted to revise it because it is such an old favorite. But to revise this one would be to write a new one. It has a lovely lilt and rhythm. But blind mice chasing a woman who cuts off their tails doesn't fit into the overall tone of this book.

Likewise, FA, FE, FI, FO, FUM (sometimes with the FA left off) is not in this book. Perhaps you will see why: "Fa, Fe, Fi, Fo, Fum! I smell the blood of an Englishman. Be he live or be he dead, I'll grind his bones to make me bread." This rhyme would need some clarification if I were to read it to my lit-

tle granddaughter, and how would I explain it?

Why is there so much violence in the early nursery rhymes? Perhaps because many of them expressed the political tensions of the day. But I don't know why someone would want to include such rhymes in collections for children. Why is there such violence on TV today for children? I don't understand the rationality of that either. I do not understand the logic of throwing violence at little children, either in nursery rhymes or on television.

Perhaps some of us are more sensitive to exposing children to violence today because of the age of violence in which we live. Or was the age when nursery rhymes were composed more of an age of violence than ours? Perhaps we merely have two standards today—one for television where vio-

lence for children is rampant and one for books where we don't tolerate a fraction of the violence we see on TV. There seems to be no logic.
What do you think?

Some of us do not want to encourage our children to drink alcohol. So this nursery rhyme was excluded, "Round about, round about, Gooseberry pie, My father loves good ale, And so do I." It isn't clear who "I" is—child or adult. It's too easy for a child to identify with the "I."

Because of cultural differences, nursery rhymes occasionally called men "pretty." There's a rhyme about pretty Bobby Shaftoe. Another speaks of two pretty men who slept together. Another begins, "Pretty John Watts, we are troubled with rats . . ." We don't commonly call men pretty today, so these rhymes were omitted.

Words and facts changed through the years in some nursery rhymes. I have an 1881 version of WEE WILLIE WINKIE that says he cried out, "Are the babes in their bed? For it's now ten o'clock." Later versions, including the one in this book, substitute "children" for "babes" and "eight o'clock" instead of "ten o'clock." Ten is a little late for younger children, isn't it?

PEASE PORRIDGE HOT was once PEASE PUDDING HOT, PEAS-PUDDING HOT, or PEAS PORRIDGE HOT. Pease is simply an old word for peas. Words have been spelled differently, too. HICKORY, DICKORY, DOCK in earlier versions was HICCORY, DICCORY, DOCK.

16

WHO WAS MOTHER GOOSE?

Mother Goose is a fictitious character who supposedly told these nursery rhymes. The idea of Mother Goose as a teller of tales is as old as a book by J. Pote in 1729.

Some say the grave of the real Mother Goose is in Boston, and that her name was Elizabeth Vergoose (or Foster Goose or Vertigoose). She was a mother of six and stepmother of ten, so she needed something to entertain her sixteen children and later her grandchildren. Her son-in-law was Thomas Fleet, and he supposedly published in 1719 the nursery rhymes which Elizabeth sang to his children (her grandchildren). But no one has ever found this book, titled SONGS FOR THE NURSERY or MOTHER GOOSE'S MELODIES. And no one knows if Elizabeth really was Mother Goose. So the origin of Mother Goose is still a mystery, but that, perhaps, makes the whole idea more delightful.

WHO ARE THE JOYFUL NOISE™ CHARACTERS?

The Joyful Noise™ characters were introduced to the public in 1992 in the book *My Bedtime Anytime Storybook*, which rose to best-seller status the same year. I was privileged to join my writing with the illustrative genius of Tim O'Connor to bring these characters to life.

So how do the Joyful Noise™ characters relate to nursery rhymes? Most nursery rhymes feature generic children, in many cases nameless and faceless, rather than children with strong character qualities. In projecting the Joyful Noise™ characters into nursery rhymes, we add two more dimensions to this book—strong characterization and a touch of humor. Look for the unusual as these characters project themselves into certain situations in a way that is sure to make your child laugh.

The adventure is ready to begin. Take classic nursery rhymes, edit slightly for children today, blend in a few new ones, add strong characters, and drop in a touch of humor and you have an evening of delight with your children or grandchildren. You will surely want to turn off the TV so you can turn on your children's imaginations.

Oh, yes, add yourself, the parent, grandparent, other family member, or teacher, and with the child, you have an unbeatable combination. No TV program on earth has something better to offer.

Now it's time to fall in love with this book. The adventure begins!

V. Gilbert Beers

Joyful Noise™
for Girls and Boys

With horns to toot
And songs to sing,
With things that clang
And some that ring,
We prance and dance
On tippy toes,

And make a happy sound
That grows.
We sing a song

For girls and boys,
So you may call us
Joyful Noise.™

Peter Piper

Peter Piper
picked
a peck
of pickled
peppers;

A peck of
pickled
peppers
Peter Piper
picked;

If Peter Piper
picked a peck
of pickled
peppers,

Where's the
peck of
pickled
peppers
Peter Piper
picked?

Classic

24

25

Humpty Dumpty

Humpty Dumpty
  sat on a wall;
Humpty Dumpty
  had a great fall;
All the king's horses,
  and all the king's men
Couldn't put Humpty Dumpty
  together again.

Classic

eggs
half price

GLUE

27

Baa, Baa, Black Sheep

Baa, baa, black sheep,
Have you any wool?
Yes sir, I have
Three bags full;

this way

One for my shepherd,
One for his wife, Jane,
And one for their little boy
Who's running
        down the lane.

Classic

31

Hot Cross Buns

Hot cross buns!
Hot cross buns!
One a penny, two a penny,
Hot cross buns!

If you have no daughters,
Give them to your sons.
One a penny, two a penny,
Hot cross buns.

Classic

On a Cold and Frosty Morning

Here we go round
The mulberry bush,
On a cold and
Frosty morning.

This is the way we
Wash our hands,
Wash our hands,
Wash our hands,

This is the way we
Wash our hands,
On a cold and
Frosty morning.

This is the way we
Wash our clothes,
Wash our clothes,
Wash our clothes,

This is the way we
Wash our clothes,
On a cold and
Frosty morning.

This is the way we
Go to school,
Go to school,
Go to school,

This is the way we
Go to school,
On a cold and
Frosty morning.

Classic

39

Seesaw

Seesaw,
Margery Daw,
Johnny shall have
A new master;

He shall have
But a penny a day,
Because he can't work
Any faster.

Classic

41

A Sunny Day Umbrella

If I put up my umbrella
on a sunny day,

Will this tell
the sun to go

And ask
the rain to stay?
V.G.B.

45

Rock-a-Bye Baby

Rock-a-bye baby,
In the tree top;
When the wind blows,
The cradle will rock;

When the bough breaks,
The cradle will fall;
Down will come baby,
Cradle, and all.

Classic

1, 2, 3, 4
One, Two, Three, Four,
and Maybe Even More

1 2

One, two,
    Tie my shoe;

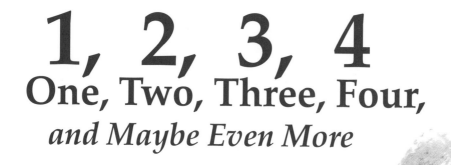

3 4

Three, four,
Knock at my door;

49

5 6

Five, six,
   Pick up sticks;

7 8

Seven, eight,
   Lay them straight;

9 10

Nine, ten,
   A big fat hen;

11 12

Eleven, twelve,
   Dig and delve;

13 14

Thirteen, fourteen,
Maids a-courting;

15 16

Fifteen, sixteen,
Maids in the kitchen;

17 18

Seventeen, eighteen,
Maids a-waiting;

19 20

Nineteen, twenty,
My plate's empty.

Classic

53

Little Boy Blue

Little Boy Blue,
Come blow your horn;
The sheep's in the meadow,
The cow's in the corn.

Where's the
little boy
That looks after
the sheep?

Under the
haystack,
Fast asleep!

Classic

55

Little Pussy

I love little Pussy,
Her coat is so warm,
And if I don't hurt her
She'll do me no harm;

So I'll not pull her tail,
Nor drive her away,
But Pussy and I
Very gently will play.

Classic

58

59

Tom, Tom, the Piper's Son

Tom, Tom, the piper's son,
Stole a pig, and away he run,

61

But the pig had feet,
And Tom was beat,
And Tom went crying down the street.

Classic

Jack Be Nimble

Jack be nimble
Jack be quick;
Jack jump over
A candlestick.

Classic

65

Helpers

Who do you need
When your tire is flat,
When your car needs a jumper
Or a brand new bumper?
Who do you need
To take care of that?

Who do you need
When you catch the flu,
When you sniffle or sneeze

Or you scratch up your knees?
Who do you need
To fix you like new?

69

Who do you need
When life begins to bend;
When things get rougher
And you start to suffer,
Who do you need
To become your Best Friend?

V.G.B.

One Misty Moisty Morning

One misty moisty morning,
When cloudy was the weather,
I met a very nice old man,
His clothes were made of leather.

He bowed and said some nice things,
And I began to grin.
"How do you do?" we both said,
And "how do you do?" again.

Classic

Teeth and Gums

Thirty-two white horses
Upon a red hill,
Now they tramp,
Now they champ,
Now they stand still.

Classic

Tears and Smiles

from Psalm 30:5

Last night I cried
When I went to bed

When I woke up,
I smiled instead.

V.G.B.

Rub a Dub Dub

Rub a dub dub,
Three men in a tub:
And who do you think they be?

The butcher, the baker,
The candlestick maker;
On their way out to sea.

Classic

83

If All the Seas Were One Sea

If all the seas were one sea,
What a GREAT sea that would be!
And if all the trees were one tree,
What a GREAT tree that would be!

And if all the axes were one axe,
What a GREAT axe that would be!
And if all the men were one man,
What a GREAT man that would be!

And if the GREAT man took the GREAT axe,
And cut down the GREAT tree,
And let it fall into the GREAT sea,
What a GREAT splash that would be.

Revised Classic

89

Little
Miss
Muffet

Little Miss Muffet
Sat on her tuffet,
Eating her curds and whey;

Along came a spider
Who sat down beside her
And frightened Miss Muffet away.

Classic

Old Mother Hubbard

Old Mother Hubbard
Went to the cupboard,
To get her poor dog
a bone;

But when she got there
The cupboard was bare,
And so the poor dog
		had none.

Classic

96

Ride a Cock-Horse

Ride a cock-horse
To Banbury Cross,
To see a fine lady
Upon a white horse;

With rings on her fingers
And bells on her toes,
She shall have music
Wherever she goes.

Classic

Coffee and Tea

Molly, my sister and I, fell out,

And what
do you think
it was all
about?

99

She loved coffee and I loved tea,

100

And that was the reason we couldn't agree.

Classic

Light Switch, Night Switch

If a light switch turns on a light,
Will a night switch turn on the night?

If I switch on the night when I want the light
Will everything turn out all right?

V.G.B.

The Yellow Butterfly

There was a yellow butterfly,
I thought I saw it flutter by.

But when I tried to say good-bye,
It fluttered up into the sky.

V.G.B.

Listen! What Do You Hear?

What makes a sound like
SNIP, SNIP, SNIP,
Snipping your hair with a
CLIPPITY CLIP?

What makes a sound like
SWISH SWISH,
Across the floor wherever
YOU WISH?

What makes a sound like
SCRUB SCRUB,

Scrubbing away in a
RUB A DUB TUB?

What makes a sound like
DING, DING, DONG,

Except when it sounds like
BONG, BONG, BONG?

115

What helps you hear sounds
FAR AND NEAR?
Thank You, God,
FOR MY WONDERFUL EARS.

V.G.B.

Thank You, God

Thank You, God, for
   a brand new day.

Two feet
   to help me run and play.

119

Two ears
   to hear what You will say.

Two eyes
    to help me walk Your way.

123

Two lips
to praise You when I pray.
V.G.B.

125

Old King Cole

Old King Cole
Was a merry
    old soul,
A merry old soul
    was he;

He called for his pipe,
And he called
    for his bowl,
And he called
    for his
    fiddlers three.

Classic

126

The King
is
IN

SOAP

A Pumpkin Pump

Do pumpkins really pump?
I think that I will try,
To make a pumpkin pump
A piece of pumpkin pie.

V.G.B.

128

Mary Had a Little Lamb

Mary had a little lamb,
Its fleece was white as snow;
And everywhere that Mary went,
The lamb was sure to go.

It followed her to school one day,
Which was against the rule.
It made the children laugh and play,
To see a lamb at school.

131

And so the teacher sent it out,
But still it lingered near,
And waited patiently about,
Till Mary did appear.

"What makes the lamb love Mary so?"
The happy children cry,
"Why, Mary loves the lamb, you know!"
The teacher did reply.

Classic

Mistakes

Bru the Bear bought some paint,
To paint his doghouse red.

But I heard him say
That his hand went astray,

And he painted his doggie instead.

V.G.B.

Wee Willie Winkie

Wee Willie Winkie
Runs through the town,
Upstairs and downstairs,
In his nightgown;

Rapping at the window,
Crying through the lock,
"Are the children in their beds?
Now it's eight o'clock."

Classic

139

The Cat and the Fiddle

Hey, diddle, diddle!
The cat and the fiddle,
The cow jumped over the moon;

NO COW JUMPING

The little dog laughed
To see such sport,
And the dish ran away with the spoon.

Classic

143

Hickory, Dickory, Dock

Hickory, dickory, dock,
A mouse ran up the clock;
The clock struck one,
The mouse ran down;
Hickory, dickory, dock.

Classic

Thirty Days Hath September

Thirty days hath September,
April, June, and November;

147

148

February has twenty-eight alone,
All the rest have thirty-one,
Excepting leap-year, that's the time
When February has twenty-nine.

Revised Classic

To Market

To market, to market, to buy a pet pig,
Home again, home again, jiggety jig.

To market, to market, to buy a pet hog,

Home again, home again, jiggety jog.

To market, to market, to buy any pet,
Home again, home again,
I won't buy it yet.

Revised Classic

Pat-a-Cake

Pat-a-cake, pat-a-cake,
Baker's man!
Make me a cake
As fast as you can.

157

Pat it, and prick it,
And mark it with P,

And put it in the oven
For Puddles and me.

Revised Classic

This Little Pig

This little pig went to market;
This little pig stayed home;
This little pig had roast beef;
This little pig had none;
This little pig said, "Wee, wee, wee!"
All the way home.

Revised Classic

161

A Star

Higher than a house,
Higher than a tree.
Oh! whatever
Can that be?

Classic

163

Goosey, Goosey, Gander

Goosey, goosey, gander,
Where do you wander?

Upstairs and downstairs
And then over yonder.

Revised Classic

166

167

Grrr

Puppies grrr,

Beaters
whirrr;

Kittens purrr,
So pet their furrr.

V.G.B.

The Robin

The north wind doth blow,
And we shall have snow,
And what will poor robin do then,
Poor thing?

171

172

He'll sit in a barn,
And keep himself warm,
And hide his head under his wing,
Poor thing.

Classic

Raindrops and Gumdrops

If raindrops were gumdrops,
God let fall from the sky,
Then I would need a gumbrella
To keep my galoshes dry.

V.G.B.

175

I Want a Pet

I want a pet,
A lion will do;

Perhaps an elephant
Or maybe two.

177

I want a pet,
That's fierce and big;

Perhaps a strong horse
Or big fat pig.

179

But since my pet
Will live in my house,
Perhaps all I need is
A little mouse.

Some pets are **BIG**
And some pets are small.
But I'm glad that God
Made them all.

V.G.B

Pussycat, Pussycat

"Pussycat, pussycat,
Where have you been?"
"I've been to London
To look at the queen."
"Pussycat, pussycat,
What did you there?"
"I frightened a little mouse
Under the chair."

Classic

183

Little Bird

Once I saw a little bird
Come hop, hop, hop.
So I cried, "Little bird,
Will you stop, stop stop?"

I was going to the window
To say, "How do you do?"
But he shook his little tail
And far away he flew.

Revised Classic

The Donkey

Donkey, donkey, old and gray,
Open your mouth and gently bray;

189

Lift your ears and blow your horn,
To wake the world this sleepy morn.

Classic

Sundaes and Mondays

Must I eat a
Chocolate sundae,
On the day
Before Monday?

Must I wait a week
To eat this treat
If I don't go
To Sundae school?

V.G.B.

193

Little Fred
Went to Bed

When little Fred
Went to bed
He always said
His prayers.

195

He kissed
His mom,

And hugged
His dad,

196

And then he went upstairs.

Revised Classic

The Little Girl with a Curl

There was a little girl who had a little curl
Right in the middle of her forehead;
When she was good, she was very, very good,
And when she was bad she was horrid.

Classic

Pease Porridge

Pease porridge hot,
Pease porridge cold,
Pease porridge in the pot,
Nine days old.

201

Some like it hot,
Some like it cold,
Some like it in the pot,
Nine days old.

Classic

The Four Seasons

Spring is the time
   for lots of showers.

205

Summer's the time
for lots of flowers.

Autumn will bring
a colorful show.

And winter's the time
for blowing snow.

Revised Classic

Peppermint Pigs
and Green Giraffes

Is a peppermint pig
Twice as big
As a licorice lion
Or two?

Is the ice cream cow
Covered now
With a chocolaty
Gooey goo?

Does a green giraffe
Try to make you laugh
As you walk through
A lollipop zoo?

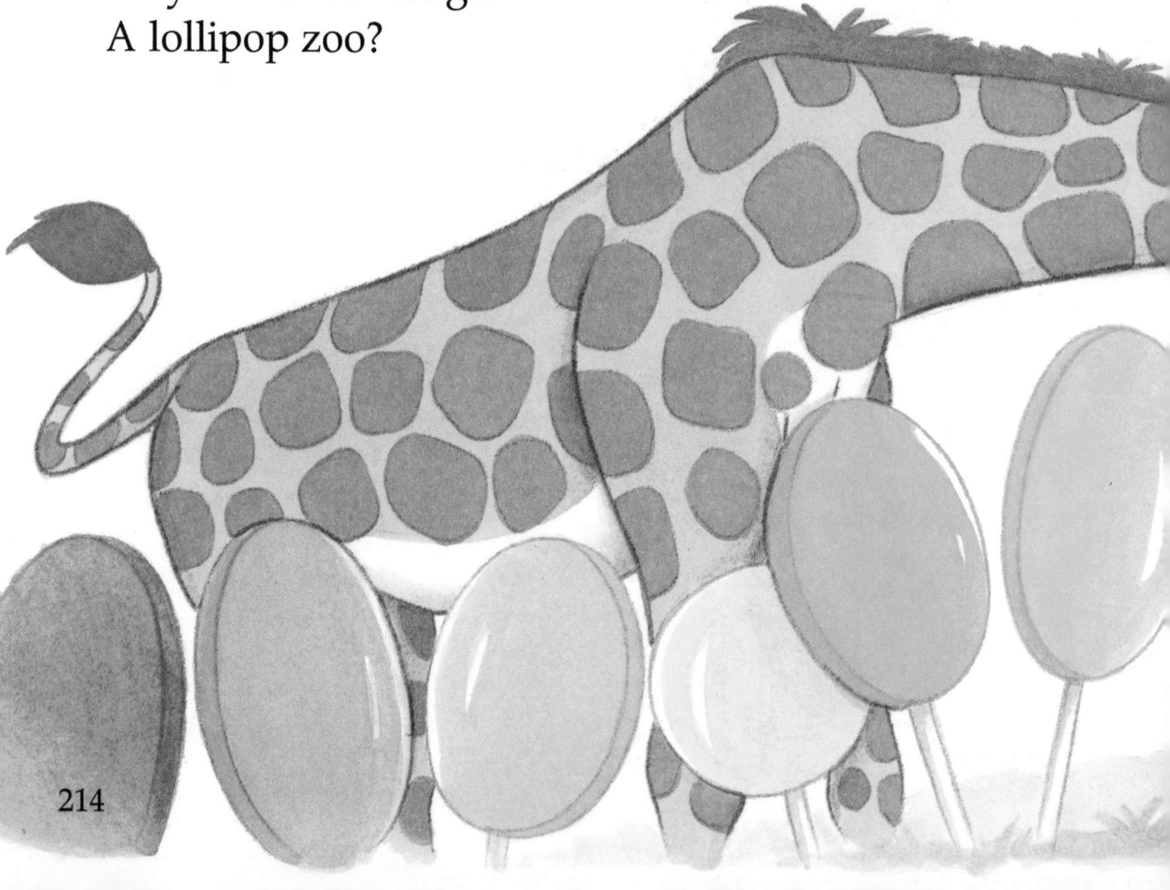

Now isn't it fun
How your mind can run?
Imagination,
What a creation!

V.G.B.

215

Snowflakes, Pancakes

If snowflakes
Were pancakes,

Then snowdrifts
Could bring tummy aches.

V.G.B.

217

Firefly

Firefly,
Flying by,
Flying high
In the sky,
Flying in the
Night sky.

219

Flash your
Flashlight,
Firefly,
So I'll
Know you're
Flying by.

V.G.B.

220

Sing a Song of Sixpence

Sing a song of sixpence,
A pocket full of rye;

Four and twenty blackbirds,
Baked in a pie.

When the pie was opened,
The birds began to sing;

Wasn't that a dainty dish,
To set before the king?

Revised Classic

Summer and Winter

Is summer the time
when spring has sprung?
Or is it the time
when fall is young?

Is winter the time when autumn is done?
Or is it the time before spring has begun?

What could be better than God's seasons?
He created each one for special reasons.

V.G.B.

Little Bo-Peep

Little Bo-Peep has lost her sheep,
And doesn't know where to find them;

Leave them alone, and they'll come home,
Dragging their tails behind them.

Revised Classic

229

Whether the Weather

Whether the weather
Brings rain or snow,

Whether the wind
Decides to blow;

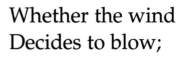

Whether it's cold,
Or whether it's hot,

I'd like the weather
To be what it's not.

Whether the weather
Is good or bad,

God makes it just right,
For that I am glad.

V.G.B.

233

Old Mother Goose

Mother Goose friends,
When they want to wander,
Will ride through the air
On a very fine gander.

Revised Classic

236

For Want of a Nail

For want of a nail, the shoe was lost;
For want of the shoe, the horse was lost;
For want of the horse, the rider was lost;

For want of the rider, the battle was lost;
For want of the battle, the kingdom was lost;

And all for the want of a horseshoe nail.

Revised Classic

Blow, Wind, Blow

Blow, wind, blow!
And go, mill, go,
So the miller may grind his corn,

241

So the baker may take it,
And into rolls make it,
And send us some hot in the morn.

Revised Classic

242

243

Fiddle-de-dee

Fiddle-de-dee, fiddle-de-dee,
The fly has married the bumblebee.
The wedding was such a sight to see,
I only wish they had invited me.

Revised Classic

244

245

My Little Hen

Hickety, pickety,
My little hen,
She lays eggs
For gentlemen;

247

Gentlemen come
Every day
To see what my
Little hen does lay.

Revised Classic

248

Rain, Rain, Go Away

Rain, rain,
  go away,
Come again
  another day;
Our friend Puddles
  wants to play.

Revised Classic

251

Little Jack Horner

Little Jack Horner,
Sat in the corner,
Eating a Christmas pie.

He put in his thumb,
And pulled out a plum,
And said, "What a good boy am I!"

Revised Classic

Mary, Mary

Mary, Mary,
Quite contrary,
How does your garden grow?

257

With silver bells,
And cockleshells,
And pretty maids all in a row.

Revised Classic

Bedtime

The Man in the Moon
Looked out of the moon,
Looked out of the moon and said,
"It's time for all
The children on earth
To think about getting to bed."

Revised Classic

261

I Saw a Ship A-Sailing

I saw a ship a-sailing,
A-sailing on the sea;
And, oh! it was all laden
With pretty things for thee!
There were chocolates in the cabin,
And apples in the hold;
The sails were made of silk,
And the masts were made of gold.

The four-and-twenty sailors
That stood between the decks,
Were four-and-twenty white mice
With scarves about their necks.
The captain was a duck,
With a packet on his back;
And when the ship began to move,
The captain said, "Quack! Quack!"

Revised Classic

265

What Would You Think?

If you saw an elephant climb a tree,
Or a snail in an eggshell go to sea,
Or a donkey drinking a cup of tea—
What would you think?

If you saw houses
upside down,

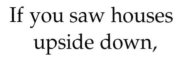

A beggar wearing
A golden crown,

268

If the stars were red and the clouds were brown—
What would you think?

Revised Classic

269

The Ten O'Clock Scholar

A dillar, a dollar, a ten o'clock scholar!
What makes you come so soon?
You used to come at ten o'clock,
But now you come at noon.

Revised Classic

271

Ding, Dong, Bell

Ding, dong, bell,
Pussy's in the well!

Who put her in?
Did Bru put her in?

Who pulled her out?
McWhiskers pulled her out.

What a naughty boy was that,
To try to hurt poor pussycat,
Who never did him any harm,
But purr in the sun, so nice and warm.

Revised Classic

275

Tom Tinker's Dog

Bow-wow-wow!
Whose dog art thou?
Little Tom Tinker's dog,
Bow-wow-wow!

Revised Classic

Jack and Jill

Jack and Jill went up the hill,
To fetch a pail of water;
Jack fell down on the hard ground,
And Jill came tumbling after.

Then up Jack got and home did trot,
As fast as he could go,
To get a patch to cover his scratch,
And that is all I know.

Revised Classic

282

A Candle

Little Miss Etticoat
In a white petticoat
And a red nose;

The longer she stands
The shorter she grows.

Revised Classic

283

A Bunch of Blue Ribbons

Oh, dear,
What can the matter be?
Johnny's so long at the fair.

He promised he'd buy me
A bunch of blue ribbons,
To tie up my pretty brown hair.

Revised Classic

Diddle, Diddle Dumpling

Diddle, diddle dumpling, my son John
Went to bed with his socks still on,
One shoe off, and one shoe on;
Diddle, diddle dumpling, my son John.

Revised Classic

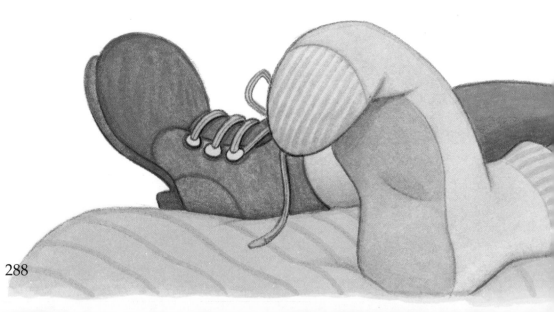

Polly, Put the Kettle On

Polly, put the kettle on,
And let's drink tea.

Sukey, take it off again,

292

They're all
gone away.

Revised Classic

293

Christmas

Christmas comes but once a year,
And when it comes it brings good cheer.

Revised Classic

Shhhh!

294

There Was an Old Woman

There was an old woman
Who lived in a shoe.

She had so many children
She didn't know what to do.

She gave them some jam
And hot buttered bread;
Then kissed them all sweetly
And tucked them in bed.

Revised Classic

299

The Crooked Sixpence

There was a crooked man,
And he went a crooked mile,
He found a crooked sixpence
And he studied it a while;

301

302

He bought a crooked cat,
Which caught a crooked mouse,
And they all lived together
In a little crooked house.

Revised Classic

Jack Sprat

Jack Sprat
Could eat no fat,

His wife
Could eat no lean;

And so, between
The two of them,

They licked the
Platter clean.

Classic

305

306

Ring Around the Rosies

Ring around the rosies,
A pocketful of posies.

Stop now! Stop now!
We all fall down.

Revised Classic

Little Bird's House

Where is your bedroom, Little Bird?
"Why, that's my nest," I thought I heard.

Where is your kitchen, Little Bird?
"Why, that's my nest," I thought I heard.

God gives you a house, Little Bird.
"And that's my nest," I thought I heard.

V.G.B.

315

It's Raining

Today I saw a flash!
And then I heard a crash!
And something then went splash!

317

Today I saw the sun!
The rain is now all done!
And now it's time for fun!

V.G.B.

318

319